This book belongs to

....

It was given to me by

....

On this date

....

DAVID & ME
Devotions for Boys

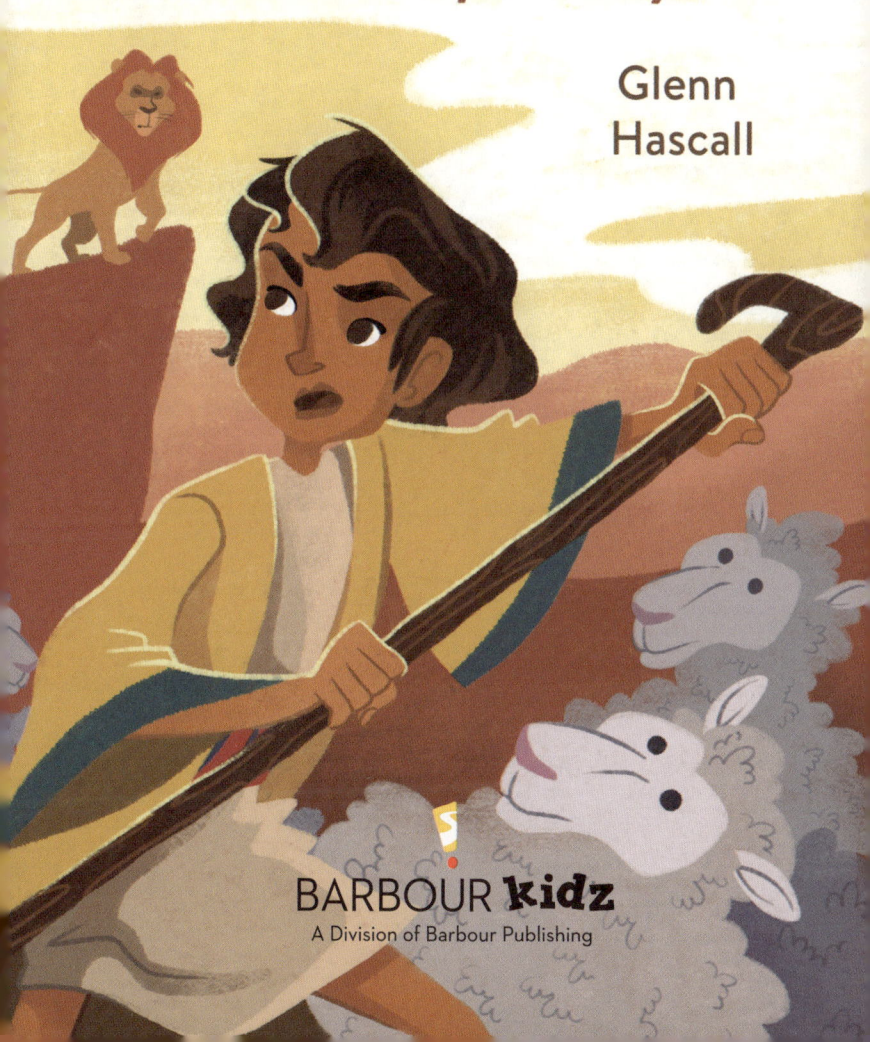

Glenn Hascall

BARBOUR kidz
A Division of Barbour Publishing

© 2023 by Barbour Publishing, Inc.

ISBN 978-1-63609-624-7

All rights reserved. No part of this publication may be reproduced or transmitted for commercial purposes, except for brief quotations in printed reviews, without written permission of the publisher. Reproduced text may not be used on the World Wide Web.

Churches and other noncommercial interests may reproduce portions of this book without the express written permission of Barbour Publishing, provided that the text does not exceed 500 words and that the text is not material quoted from another publisher. When reproducing text from this book, include the following credit line: "From *David & Me: Devotions for Boys*, published by Barbour Publishing, Inc. Used by permission."

Scripture quotations marked SKJV are taken from the Barbour Simplified KJV, copyright © 2022 by Barbour Publishing, Inc., Uhrichsville, Ohio 44683. All rights reserved.

Scripture quotations marked NLV are taken from the New Life Version, copyright © 1969 and 2003 by Barbour Publishing, Inc., Uhrichsville, Ohio 44683. All rights reserved.

Scripture quotations marked NIV are taken from the HOLY BIBLE, NEW INTERNATIONAL VERSION®. NIV®. Copyright © 1973, 1978, 1984, 2011 by Biblica, Inc.™ Used by permission. All rights reserved worldwide.

Cover illustrations by Pedro Riquelme

Published by Barbour Publishing, Inc., 1810 Barbour Drive, Uhrichsville, Ohio 44683, www.barbourbooks.com

Our mission is to inspire the world with the life-changing message of the Bible.

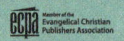

Printed in China.

001651 0723 DS

Welcome to
DAVID & ME
Devotions for Boys!

Turn these pages and you'll read words. Those words will take you on an adventure in the life of David. He was a shepherd. He was a king. He was even a very young champion against a nine-foot-tall man of war. He was a famous author. He worked to make things right and spent enough time remembering God's goodness that He found it hard not to be thankful.

You have lots of dreams. Some are big, and others you'll probably finish before your next meal. Are any of them God's dreams? That's a question David wanted to know the answer to. His big dreams were always introduced by God. David was a leader who followed, a dreamer who cared what God thought, and a boy who understood sheep.

Keep turning the pages. Keep reading! There's more to learn on a great adventure. That adventure starts today.

SHEPHERD BOY

THE FORGOTTEN SON

Samuel said to Jesse, "Are all your children here?" And he said, "There still remains the youngest, and behold, he is keeping the sheep."

1 SAMUEL 16:11 SKJV

David was busy watching sheep play on the hillside. His home was not very close. He would have to walk a long time before he got home. His job was to stay with the sheep and make sure nothing happened to them. He took his job seriously. So he learned new things about sheep every day.

What David didn't know was that in his family home there was a man named Samuel. This man of God had been sent by God to help find Israel's next king. Samuel spoke with David's seven brothers, who were all at home. But he couldn't find the one God wanted to make king.

David's dad, Jesse, had forgotten about David. Maybe it was because he was the youngest. When Samuel asked if there were any more sons, Jesse remembered David. But bringing David to the house would take time. It would take a long walk to find him and a long walk to bring him back. But Jesse sent for him. This shepherd boy would be the next king.

You may feel like the least important person in your family, but God knows you better than anyone. He can do something with you that no one thought possible. Let Him do that.

*Surprise me, Lord. When
I understand Your plan,
make me brave enough to
follow where You lead.*

NO NEED FOR FEAR

David said to [King] Saul, "Your servant was taking care of his father's sheep."

1 Samuel 17:34 NLV

It was dark outside, but that was part of the job. The sheep went *baa* around him. But David couldn't help looking at the stars. He leaned on his shepherd's staff and hummed a song he had made up. The sheep seemed to listen. But it wasn't long before the sheep were afraid.

Just beyond the light of the campfire, David saw two eyes glow in the darkness. Then he heard a growl. David knew what to do. He stood up, and the sheep got behind him. The staff he carried became a weapon. He would use it to make the bear or lion go away. God was with David. And David followed God. The sheep would be safe. David learned a big lesson when he was very small. God is bigger than darkness and scary growls. He's stronger than young boys and big bears. He's wiser than sheep and kings.

This shepherd wasn't much older than you. David used his time with sheep to learn from God. What he knew for sure was that *no one* is bigger than God.

Do you ever wonder if God is real? Do you believe that He takes care of you? Do you ever ask for His help?

I can get scared like a sheep, God. Help me to remember that You're bigger than what frightens me—and You aren't afraid of anything.

LEARNING TO OBEY

Jesse said to his son David, "Take for your brothers a basket of this baked grain and these ten loaves. Hurry and carry them to your brothers among the army."

1 Samuel 17:17 NLV

David was going to be king. But he was asked to stay with the sheep while his older brothers became soldiers. Maybe David felt sorry for himself. If he did, it got worse when his father, Jesse, asked him to carry food to his brothers.

The Bible doesn't say if David was sad or not. It does say that he obeyed Jesse. He left the sheep in the care of someone else and walked to the place where soldiers gathered for battle. The Bible doesn't say if David got any of the food. It does say that he took the ten loaves of bread to his brothers.

It was important for David to learn to obey. God would ask him to do some very hard things in the years ahead. It would not be helpful if David said no. So, first, David had to learn to obey his father. Then it became easier to obey God.

Maybe you've heard that God wants you to obey your parents. He wanted the same thing for a king. Obedience must be very important to God.

David was once a boy like me, Father. If it was important for him to obey, then help me to remember I should do the same.

BATTLING GOLIATH

WHO'S THAT MAN?

All the men of Israel, when they saw the man, fled from him and were greatly afraid.

1 Samuel 17:24 SKJV

Jesse watched his son David, and it made him think about his older sons. They were soldiers. They were with the king on a mountainside. There they faced a group of men called the Philistines. Jesse wondered how they were doing. That's why he sent David to take them some food and find out what he could.

So David went. He learned that his brothers and the rest of Israel's soldiers were up against a nine-foot-tall soldier named Goliath. This huge Philistine stood on the other side of the valley. From there he called Israel's soldiers bad names. David knew that wasn't right. Why didn't Israel's soldiers make him stop? David learned that Goliath scared everyone—including his brothers.

You might get scared too when you don't know how to do something that seems hard. You think you might be in trouble. You might even know what needs to be done but think you aren't strong enough to do it well.

David had seen fear before. The sheep he cared for were scared—a lot. But hadn't he stood up to lions and bears? Hadn't God been with him? Hadn't God kept the sheep safe? Would God also protect the soldiers of His own army?

The people needed a hero. David knew that God would send one.

When things seem too big
for me, Lord, help me to
remember they're no struggle
for You. Remind me that
You can make me strong.

GOD IS WITH YOU

David said, "The Lord Who saved me from the foot of the lion and from the foot of the bear, will save me from the hand of this Philistine." Saul said to David, "Go, and may the Lord be with you."

1 Samuel 17:37 NLV

David was taken to King Saul. He offered to do what no soldier had done. He would face Goliath. And young David was sure he'd win.

The king remembered what David had done to protect sheep. Maybe Saul wondered if God would use David's trust in Him to win the battle.

The king wanted to protect David. But the armor he offered was too big, the sword too long, and the shield too heavy. How could a boy fight a man's battle without armor? David knew God could protect him. If the battle could be won, God would need to protect David.

He wasn't a regular soldier. David was a volunteer, someone who offers to do a job he doesn't have to do. Other soldiers must have thought it was strange to see a boy walking out of the camp toward the enemy. But David knew God was with him.

God never says you have to be old to do big, important things. You can do them now—with His help. Just be sure to tell others that God gives you the strength.

*I want to be a volunteer, God.
Help me to say yes to You.
Then do big things through me.*

GOD IS BIGGER THAN ANYTHING

The Philistine said to David, "Am I a dog, that you come to me with sticks?"

1 Samuel 17:43 NLV

David had a big job to do. He wanted to beat this Philistine giant, who was used to winning battles. David left the camp with a sling, a weapon that was used to throw stones. He also carried five smooth stones he found in a creek.

Some people thought he was foolish. David's brothers thought he was showing off. Yet everyone waited to see what would happen. Here was a boy who wasn't a soldier facing a man who frightened every soldier of Israel.

Goliath thought David was wasting his time. David told the big Philistine that he had picked a fight with God. And David told Goliath that God would win. With his slingshot and one stone, David did just that. The boy knocked down the giant and killed him!

David learned when he was very young that God is bigger than anything that frightened him. You should learn that too. Things can seem too big and too scary—but when you believe God takes care of you, you'll be very brave.

You might never send me to face a real giant, Father. But You might ask me to face hard things and to let You help me. That's just what I need to do.

HOW GOOD IS GOD?

[King] Saul sent to Jesse, saying, "Let David, I ask you, stand before me, for he has found favor in my sight."

1 Samuel 16:22 skjv

David had learned about sheep. He was learning about God. As he sat with the sheep, he even learned to play music about God. The Bible doesn't say how people found out David could play. But when King Saul needed someone to make music to cheer him up, David was the person people talked about.

David wasn't yet a soldier. He was too young. But he went to work in King Saul's court. Saul liked David and often asked him to play music for him.

David wrote many of the psalms. So maybe he was writing new words and music even as a boy. First he might have played to sheep. Later he played music for a king. He used his music to sing of God's goodness. Music would be important to David for the rest of his life.

Do you like to sing? If you do, sing songs to God! Even if you don't like to sing, you can *tell* God what you're grateful for. Write things down and read them to Him the next time you pray.

*It's easy to forget how good
You are, Father. Help me to
remember and use words
to tell You all about it.*

SONGS THAT HELP

David took a harp and played music with his hand. So Saul was refreshed and was well.

1 Samuel 16:23 skjv

David was growing up. He wasn't a king yet. But God had promised that he would be. And God always keeps His promises. One day God *would* make David the king. And Saul couldn't do anything to stop it.

But while David waited, he also helped the king. The king wanted David to play music for him. The music made the king feel better. David did not want to be king before God said it was time. So while he waited, he treated King Saul kindly.

David used music to praise God, tell

stories of victory, and show sadness. King Saul would listen to these songs. So would everyone who was with the king. David wanted these songs to be truthful. They could make people feel happy or sad. They still can today.

Did you know that music is one way you can honor God? You might play an instrument, sing a song, or listen to someone else. When those songs honor God, it's a very good thing. Like David, you can choose songs that help.

Music can help me remember important things about You, Lord. Help me to use songs to remember that You're good and love me very much.

SERVING KING SAUL

SELFISH SAUL

The women sang as they played, and said, "Saul has killed his thousands, and David his ten thousands."

1 Samuel 18:7 NLV

David helped King Saul. He always had. Saul made David a leader in the army. David was such a good leader that the people chose something like a parade to honor the good work David was doing. They shouted in the streets. And the words they used made David seem more important than the king. Saul didn't like that.

David had not asked to be honored. And he still wanted to help the king. But King Saul was angry with David. He even tried to hurt the young man.

The people saw that God was making

David brave and strong. But Saul looked less brave and less strong. Saul seemed to think David was trying to become king. Saul was afraid and angry. He didn't want anyone to be more important than him.

It can be easy to think bad thoughts about people who get more attention than you do. You might try to make others think the other person isn't good—that you are better than he is. God doesn't want you to do that. Do the best job you can. Let God choose whether it gets a "well done."

Help me pay attention to the choices I make, Father. I don't need to think about what other people do. I just want to do my best for You.

WHY WAS SAUL SO ANGRY?

Saul saw and knew that the L<small>ORD</small> was with David. . . . And Saul became David's enemy continually. . . . David behaved more wisely than all the servants of Saul.

1 S<small>AMUEL</small> 18:28–30 <small>SKJV</small>

King Saul didn't want David to take his job. David wanted to be Saul's friend. But Saul thought everyone was an enemy. David did his best to help the king. The king did what he could to hurt David.

One day, David was writing a song. You can still read his words in your Bible, in Psalm 57. David's words told how he felt when the king was mean. David wrote, "Show me loving-kindness, O God, show me loving-kindness. For my soul goes to You to be safe. . .until the trouble has passed" (verse 1 NLV).

It can be very hard when you want to help people. But they treat you as if you're making their lives worse. It can be hard to be kind and have people think you've treated them badly. It can be hard to show love and be hated in return. Those things happened to David. They might happen to you. But God says you should still be helpful, kind, and loving.

You can't change the way others act, but you can make good choices for yourself.

*When people are mean,
I don't have to make the
same choice, God. Help me
to do what You say is best,
even when others don't.*

REMEMBER WHAT GOD HAS DONE

The priest said, "The sword of Goliath the Philistine, whom you slew in the Valley of Elah, behold, it is wrapped here in a cloth. . . . If you will take that, take it. For there is no other here except that."

1 SAMUEL 21:9 SKJV

It had been many years since David faced the giant and won. David had experienced other hard days too. He was chased by men who didn't like him. His only safe place seemed to be when he spoke to God.

Maybe that's why David went to see a priest, a man who served God. David was hungry. The priest gave him food. David needed protection too. So the priest brought the sword that David had won from the giant Goliath.

David remembered his battle with

Goliath. He also remembered things like sheep, bears, and lions. He remembered soldiers, armor, and living in tents in the field. And David remembered that God had been with him in everything he had gone through.

Every day you're growing bigger, and every day you can become wiser. God did big things for David, and He's done big things for you. You just have to remember those things. When you do, thank Him for what He's done for you.

I'm not sure my story will ever be as big and important as David's, God. And his story is not as big as Yours! Thanks for making my story a good one.

WHAT WOULDN'T DAVID DO?

[David said to King Saul,] "Your eyes have seen how the Lord gave you to me today in the cave. Some told me to kill you, but I had pity on you. I said, 'I will not put out my hand against my leader, for he is the Lord's chosen one.'"

1 Samuel 24:10 nlv

King Saul chased David away. Many of Saul's soldiers followed David. He had once been a champion for the king. Now the king thought David was the enemy.

One night Saul entered a cave. He didn't know David and his soldiers were hiding there. Each soldier must have held his breath, hoping the king wouldn't hear him. David crawled up to Saul. He quietly cut off a corner of the king's robe before Saul left the cave. That showed the king that David could have captured him—but made the better choice. David wanted the king to understand that he wasn't an enemy. Later he told the king that he would not do anything to hurt him.

This is hard to understand. When people are mean to us, it's easy to be mean back to them. God wanted David to be kind even when he had the chance to be mean. Most people don't live that way. But it's what God wanted for David. It's what He wants for you too.

I want what I do to others to look like what You do for me, Lord. Help me to include kindness and helpfulness in every choice.

KING OF ISRAEL

REMEMBERED FOR WISDOM

David behaved wisely in all his ways, and the LORD was with him.

1 SAMUEL 18:14 SKJV

David is remembered for making a lot of great choices. People thought he was a wise king.

He didn't make perfect choices. But most of the time he asked what God wanted him to do before he made a decision.

When he didn't ask God first, his choices were often wrong. But even when he broke God's rules, David came back to God quickly. Then he admitted that God was right and he was wrong. God even said that David pleased him. When David became king, he made sure God was welcome in Israel and that the people would know they should follow Him. David did his best to make God famous. Because David honored God, the people followed his example.

You can be a wise example for others too. Follow God. Make Him welcome in everything you do. And trust that His wisdom is always just right for you. If you break God's law, do what David did. Don't wait—admit that you were wrong and He was right.

Wouldn't it be great to be remembered for being wise?

Help me to be wise like David, Father. Help me to listen to You and do what You say. May I always come back to You quickly if I wander away.

WINNING JERUSALEM

David had said, "Anyone who conquers the Jebusites will have to use the water shaft to reach...David's enemies."

2 SAMUEL 5:8 NIV

David finally became king. He ruled over the land of Judah, the southern part of Israel. Then he became king of all Israel. The best place to rule both parts of the country from was the city of Jebus, also called Jerusalem. But people called Jebusites, who did not know God, lived there. So God helped David win this city.

The Jebusites believed David could *never* take their city. Even their blind people and those who couldn't walk would fight him off, they said.

But David knew about a tunnel that brought water into the city. He planned to enter the city through the tunnel and win Jerusalem for Israel.

The brave soldier Joab went first, quietly stepping through the water in the tunnel. Other soldiers followed him. When they reached the end of the tunnel, they rushed into the city and won the battle.

Then the new king ruled his people from Jerusalem. Soon it was called "the city of David."

God helped David. He wants to help you do good things too. He may not ask you to fight a war. But He always wants you to follow Him.

*Lord, please help me
do amazing things
through faith in You.*

ASK GOD FIRST

Then David asked the Lord, "Should I go up against the Philistines? Will You give them into my hand?" And the Lord said to David, "Go up, for it is sure that I will give the Philistines into your hand."

2 Samuel 5:19 NLV

The Philistines heard that David was now king of Israel. None of them had forgotten the day the shepherd boy killed their hero, Goliath. They remembered when David became the leader of King Saul's army. One time, he led his men against the Philistines in battle. The Philistines were frightened and ran away from David's stronger army.

Now that he was king, David was an even bigger danger to the Philistines. So their army leaders decided to act right away. The soldiers grabbed their swords and shields and went to a valley near David's city, Jerusalem. They wanted to fight things out fast!

David saw his enemies. But he wasn't afraid. The king knew what to do when trouble came near—he prayed and asked God if he should fight. God promised David that he and his men would win the battle. So they trusted God and went to war.

The Israelites won the battle. God was faithful to David.

God will be faithful to you too. Just be sure that you ask Him what you should do *before* you do it. Then do what He says.

Thank You for keeping Your promises to me, Lord. Help me to ask You what I need to do every day.

A SPECIAL BOX

They brought in the special box of the Lord and put it in its place inside the tent David had set up for it. And David gave burnt gifts and peace gifts to the Lord. When he had finished giving the burnt gifts and peace gifts, David prayed that good would come to the people in the name of the Lord of All.

2 SAMUEL 6:17–18 NLV

Hundreds of years before David, Moses led the Israelites through the wilderness to the land God had promised them. This story was shared from parents to children, over and over again, down through the years.

After he became king of Israel, David thought about the story. He remembered part of the story told about a special box, called the ark of the covenant. It had been made to hold two pieces of flat stone called tablets that God gave Moses. God had written the Ten Commandments on those tablets.

David left with a huge crowd of men to go to the town where the ark was. With cheering and joy, David brought the special box home to Jerusalem. This honored God and reminded the people to trust in Him.

You can honor God by reading His Word, the Bible. You can tell other people about the good things God has done for you. You can sing songs that honor Him. When you share God with others, they might want to follow Him too.

Let me follow You with cheering and joy, God. May other people see You in what I do.

"I WANT TO BUILD A TEMPLE"

[God said to David,] "I was with you wherever you went, and have cut off all your enemies out of your sight and have made you a great name, similar to the name of the great men who are on the earth."

2 Samuel 7:9 skjv

Everyone thought it was a good idea for King David to build a temple for God. That's a big stone building where God could be worshipped. But God had another idea. He reminded David that He had lived in a big tent called the "tabernacle" since the people left Egypt with Moses. God would have a temple built—just not yet.

God never made David feel bad for wanting to build the temple. God even promised that David's son would build it. David needed to remember that even without a temple God had always been with him. God wanted the king to know that he could still worship without a fancy building.

It was enough for David to know that God was always with him. God hadn't left yet and He wouldn't be leaving.

You don't have to go to a building on Sunday to be with God. He is with you all the time! It doesn't matter where you go because He never leaves. And He never gives up. He's your friend and He will never pretend that He's not.

No matter where I am, You're there, Lord. You're with me and You always will be. Thank You.

A BETTER PATH

Mephibosheth the son of Saul's son Jonathan came to David. . . . David said to him, "Do not be afraid. For I will be sure to show kindness to you because of your father Jonathan. I will return to you all the land of your grandfather Saul. And you will eat at my table always."

2 SAMUEL 9:6–7 NLV

David had a wonderful friend named Jonathan. He was King Saul's son, and he and David saw each other often in the palace. But Jonathan died in a battle before David became king.

After he became king, David wanted to do something good for Jonathan's family. Saul had wanted to kill David. But Jonathan had loved David and helped his friend escape from danger. Jonathan's son Mephibosheth was disabled. King David wanted to show his love for Jonathan, so he had his men search for the boy. Then

David asked him to come to his palace. He gave Mephibosheth Saul's lands and made him welcome any time.

David could have hated Saul's whole family. But the new king knew that wasn't what God wanted him to do. It wouldn't have been good for the kingdom. And it would have made David's heart very hard. So he took a better path by loving Mephibosheth.

Like David, we can be kind to people instead of staying angry. God can heal the hurts we feel. We don't hate people when He puts forgiveness in our hearts.

Lord, help me know how to forgive instead of hating.

WHY WE REMEMBER DAVID

PRAYER AND PRAISE

*O L̲ᴏʀᴅ our Lord, how excellent
is Your name in all the earth!*

Psalm 8:9 skjv

About half of the Bible's book of Psalms was written by David. In the psalms you'll read poems, prayers, and praises. All three were important to a shepherd-king who learned about God while working with sheep on a hillside. He wrote his songs, poems, and prayers while sheep ate grass, played, and slept. He trusted God when bears and lions came to try to steal lambs.

As a king, David kept learning what God wanted and remembering the Lord's goodness. He kept writing new songs. We don't know the tunes David used, but his songs are still sung today with new music. David isn't remembered for one special prayer or one really nice praise song. He's remembered for many psalms that brought him closer to God. Those psalms are still helping people to know God today.

David encouraged people to pray and praise together. Somehow it strengthens each person who does that.

Just look at Psalm 8:9. The name *Lord* means God is the one in charge. Having the most excellent name in all the earth means that no one will ever be more important. Take this wisdom and make it your best thought of the day. Then you will have learned something pretty wonderful.

Help me choose to pray to You and praise You, God. I need to talk with You. I need to remember Your love for me.

DAVID'S MOST IMPORTANT RELATIVE

The Good News was promised long ago by God's early preachers in His Holy Writings. It tells of His Son, our Lord Jesus Christ, Who was born as a person in the flesh through the family of King David.

ROMANS 1:2–3 NLV

Jesus is God's Son. He came to rescue people who sinned and knew they couldn't rescue themselves.

Jesus was born into King David's family many years after David died. Jesus' mother, Mary, came from King David's family line. David is remembered for following the God who later sent His Son to save people's souls. People today are like the sheep David cared for.

Every person faces tough times. Everyone needs peace and hope. That's what Jesus offers to anyone who will follow Him. David didn't know everything about Jesus, who was born a thousand years later. But David knew that God was going to do something special through one of his relatives.

God knows everything. He knew that one day boys like you would look back at the life of David. And through him you can learn more about Jesus. Jesus was what David really wanted to be like. Until Jesus came, David was one of the best examples of a person who follows God.

Take all the stuff you've learned about David and be brave, thankful, and wise. Follow God through Jesus. Allow Him to lead you. You'll never go wrong!

I have lots to think about, God. You have lots to teach. Please help me to learn. You lead, and I'll follow!